Praise for Islanders

Blending research and imagination, Teow Lim Goh creates a polyphonic narrative of early twentieth-century Chinese immigrants who were detained on Angel Island. In these spare but powerful lyrics, she presents fragments of the same material from disparate points of view, and then provides a backgrounding flashback to 1877 San Francisco, where "the Chinese must go" becomes a refrain. In this poignant journey across "the borders we inhabit, the borders / we inherit," the author finds a history that she makes ours, as well as her own.

— **Martha Collins, author of *Blue Front* and *White Papers***

The voices channeled by Teow Lim Goh in Islanders arrive with little poetic adornment, with a restraint instilled by Chinese culture and reinforced by exile and imprisonment. It is possible to fee rage while hearing, or overhearing, these distress calls from the forgotten reaches of American history. But the real power of this poetry sings out from an empathy so complete that we readers and the poet herself almost vanish into them. Instead of cultural difference and the exile of history, Goh's poetry reminds us that the suffering these poems give voice to exists here and now, in the forgotten reaches of our own lives.

—**Joseph Hutchison, Colorado Poet Laureate, author of *Thread of the Real* and *Marked Men***

These poems are imagined out of ash—script written on walls of a detention building that burned down and took the record with it. Teow Lim Goh would have those voices back, voices from the barracks, voices at the gates, on sea crossings to China, on bay crossings to San Francisco, amid riots and in cold examination rooms, in a brothel, in a prison shower, in rooms of privilege and power, challenging readers to navigate layered tone and intersubjectivity, all of it staged at the theatre of lost history, recovered.

— **Chris Ransick, author of *Language for the Living and the Dead***

Teow Lim Goh's important first collection of poems gives voice to the Chinese immigrants detained on Angel Island during the Chinese exclusionary era. Like the sea "spinning a song of solitude and pain," these poems are haunting, deliberate, and utterly relevant to contemporary issues of race and immigration. Goh's work is fearless: like the imprisoned women on the island, these poems "never return and never arrive." Instead, they reverberate with the unanswerable question, "why must I prove that I am me?"

— Nancy Pearson, author of *The Whole by Contemplation of a Single Bone*

In between seeing and saying. In between shadow and fire. The voices and words in Islanders honor the bodies of women disappeared from history, reminding us how it is that America has always been standing on the bodies of those it swallowed whole. In the lost voices of Chinese women detained at Angel Island we have the chance to yet hear something from the ruins: song.

— Lidia Yuknavitch, author of *The Small Backs of Children*

Islanders

Islanders

Teow Lim Goh

CONUNDRUM PRESS
AN IMPRINT OF BOWER HOUSE
DENVER

 Bower House books may be purchased with bulk discounts for educational, business, or sales promotional use. For information, contact Bower House P.O. Box 7459 Denver, CO 80207 or visit BowerHouseBooks.com.

Printed in Canada.

ISBN: 978-1-942280-31-6
Library of Congress Control Number: 2016939805

10 9 8 7 6 5 4 3 2

For those who inhabit the borderlands.

"The road to paradise often runs through prison."
Rebecca Solnit

"And we listen for what the waves intone."
Natasha Trethewey

Table of Contents

ANGEL ISLAND

13

★

VOICES

Angel Island, 1910 – 1940

17

ECHOES

San Francisco, 1910 – 1940

33

WORK

Angel Island, 1910 – 1940

45

RIOT

San Francisco, July & August 1877

59

★

PILGRIMAGE

77

★

NOTES

81

Angel Island

To the miners who sailed the Pacific
with dreams of golden rivers.
To the workers who built the railroads
over mountains and prairie skies.
To the farmers who made the desert bloom.

To the Chinese who were attacked
for the color of their skins.
To the aliens who posed as citizens,
their papers lost, a quake and fire.
To the paper sons who forged a history.

To the detainees on an island
between the sea and the sky.
To the poets who penned on barrack walls
songs of hope and hazy dreams,
sobs of home and nights alone.

To the paper sons who began new lives
under assumed names,
anxious their ruse would be unmasked,
afraid to tell their children
of their past.

This is not my history.
I am not the daughter of a miner.
I am not the daughter of a laborer.
I am not the daughter of a farmer.
I am not the daughter of a
paper son
false citizen
prisoner.
This is not my legacy.

This is my history.
I crossed the sea.
I sat on a plane.
I came with the dream
        of freedom
                to speak
                        to believe.
It is here I begin to write.
This is my legacy.

Voices

Angel Island, 1910 to 1940

IN A WOODEN BUILDING

So I wait on Angel Island,
this island of immortals.
The grass is dry and golden,
waves scour the headlands,
and the sea churns around me.
The children now a year older,
a year beyond their father,
another year without me.
Each day we knit in silence,
socks for the children,
hats for the parents,
and our words swirl in the sea.

A brush and a bottle of ink.
I took them when he died.
He loved to write.
What would he say if he were me?

I open the bottle.

I dip in the brush.

I write on the walls.

I tell the story of a widow
            alone in a prison at sea.
I tell the story of long nights
            wanting my children with me.
I imagine him in heaven,
I write to forget the tedium,
and maybe one day you'll remember me.

THE WAVES

His father died
suddenly, leaving a sick wife
and four young girls.
He decided to go to America, stake
a claim on Golden Mountain,
and come back for me.

He wrote to me
of Angel Island, where officers
scrutinized his papers
and doctors
made him stand naked
as they inspected
his eyes. He built a business
selling groceries,
sent money home, and came back
to marry me.

I threw up on
the sea. He calmed me,
made love to me.
The first time I cried
silently. I had not been
with another man, but I knew
he had a woman.
What could I do? There was
no land in sight.

San Francisco.
The green hills
of late spring on the verge

of a golden splendor. The city
rose from the sea
veiled in a hazy blue.
They let him land
from the ship but I had to board
a ferry. They didn't even
let us say goodbye.

There's nothing
we can do. Foreign wife
of a Chinese merchant, your case
is automatically
denied.

At night I watch
the sea. I want its embrace,
cold, dangerous, overwhelming –
in these waves
I will finally be home.

BETWEEN THE SEA AND SKY

They found her in a pool of blood,
a sharpened chopstick in her ear.
I don't even know her name.

She came with two boys,
one her son, the other an actor,
to join her husband in California,

but their case was denied.
After she died, Washington gave
the orders to land the boys.

⋆

A matron found her hanging
and cut the rope. She was alive.
The baby inside her stirred.

She went back to China with
her infant son. On their return,
the officers refused to let them land.

The boy got sick and died.
Her husband came to get the body,
appealed to Washington

to let her bury the boy.
But the decision came: *Denied.*
No unusual hardship found.

⋆

In the bathroom we now watch
for each other. Each time someone
is there with me,

I avert my eyes from hers.
There's too much that isn't said.
There's too much that cannot be said.

SCRUTINY

How far is your village
from the railway station?

Where is the rice bin
in your family home?

Who paid for your passage
to America?

Why must I answer
these questions?

When can I join my love
in the land of the free?

Why do I live
in a wooden building?

Why must I prove
that I am me?

THE WALLS SPEAK

The year I turned fourteen,
Father took me out of school.

I scrubbed the floors,
washed the clothes.

At night, by candlelight,
I snuck in my brother's books,

dreaming of a faraway land
where I could read and write.

*

Here the fog obscures
the full moon and the stars.

The sea spins a song
of solitude and pain.

I wait for my turn to enter
the land of the free.

At night, by candlelight,
I write in a notebook I hide.

*

On the walls I see poems,
brushed in ink, carved on wood,

laments of lost women
stumbling in the world.

I read their stories
and weep.

*

Each time
I pick up the knife,

ready to etch my words
into the wood,

my hands tremble
and I step back.

*

At night I lie awake.
Will I always be a secret?

ON THE BOAT

A fish tank in his room.

No fish,
only seaweed and water.

I imagined guppies
circling the glass, nowhere to go.

We knew we would part
in San Francisco.

I did not love him,
but for the first time in my life

I felt held.
These things I am not supposed to know.

Some nights I wonder where
he is.

VIRTUE EXAM

Their voices blister my skin.
Denied. She must be a whore.
My face burns. I want to hide.
I am a wife, on my way home.

IN NAME ONLY

Tomorrow
I'll cross the bay.
I'll leave the past behind,
take on another name,
and marry another man.
I've seen only his picture.
He's twenty years older.
But I have no choice.
The drought came,
the crops died.
A man in America
is the only way out.
Now my life will always be
an act.

LANDED

I want to forget this island
where waves drown
those who dream of escape.

I will never look back.

But I know that in my dreams
I'll see our words on the walls,
touch the blood on the floor,

feel the fog on my skin,
smell the salt of the breeze.
I know that wherever I go

I will carry this island with me.

IN THE ASHES

I was asleep
They rang the alarm
Flames scorched my feet
I scuttled downstairs
The sky lit up red
Smoke singed my skin
The wooden walls crackled
Our words lost in the blaze

Echoes

San Francisco, 1910 to 1940

A RETURN TO SHORE

From the beginning I knew
we would part.

You are like a bird –

Hold you by your wings
and I find feathers in my hands.

Hold you by your feet
and I find me drowning at sea.

The waves carry in a broken seashell.

I run a finger on its edge.

I fill it with the sea.

LETTER UNSENT

My dear bride,

A year has passed and I have failed
to get you to shore. The fault is mine.
I know what it's like in that prison,
an island neither land nor water, not
knowing if or when you can land.
I've been there. Twenty years ago
I sailed the Pacific, dreaming of
mountains and rivers running gold.
I landed in that prison instead, trying
to prove my name, my family, my
humanity. But my father had died,
my mother needed money. I left a girl
behind. I built a grocery business,
made enough to bring her to me,
but the law changed when we were
at sea. Foreign wife of a merchant,
she could not be landed. She went
home, never the same again. For years
I thought I could not love again.
Then my friend, your uncle, told me
about you, his sister's girl. Your father
left, your mother needed money. I
thought I could save you, give you
everything I never had. How wrong
I am. You are still young. I'm the ruin
of the man I had once been. Maybe
I have said too much.

FOR THE CHILDREN

Six months I waited
on that island, not knowing

if or when I could land. We wrote
on the walls, over

the paint and putty they used
to erase our words,

our verses etched on those
that came before. I copied them

into a notebook
that I hid. I still have it, but

I cannot bear to open it,
relive the dread

and the shame. I want to give it
to our children

after we're gone, tell them
who we are, who we once were.

CONSOLATION

They told me you died
of causes unknown.
The ink on the letter
still bleeds.
But I know you stuck a
chopstick in your ear,
writhed all night
on the floor.
What could I have done
to help you,
give you hope,
bring you home?
I shouldn't have brought in
the other boy.
It's my fault.
The boys
are with me now.
What do I say
when they ask,
where did Mother go?

AT THE BROTHEL

I wait here
for you to arrive, my wife.
I'm counting the days
before they let you
come to shore.
I can already hear
the voices
of our children,
see their tiny feet
playing in the sand.
You would never forgive me
if you knew.
But what can I say?
At night I lie awake,
alone, wanting
the comfort of home.

PAPER SON

I haven't told you
my name is not my own,
but one I took
when I came to America,
telling those people
I was the son
of a man I never knew.
When you marry me
you'll have to learn
the secrets,
what to call me at home,
what name we use outside.

AVENGE DREAM

How dare they say that
about you.

If I ever see them
I'll spit in their eyes,

slap them
with my shoe.

AS YOU WAKE

They say they found you
hanging, the bones broken

in your neck. They say
I cannot see you yet,

but at night
I think of you -

tying the rope to the ceiling
your eyes unmoving

wailing at the officer
wanting to bury our boy

dappling his body with water
trying to calm his chills

not yet knowing
another child's in you.

TOMORROW

I will come early
and wait for your ferry.

I will hug you and never let you go.

I will bring you home to a feast.

No matter
how far I must walk,

no matter
the shadows in the sky,

I will be there for you.

But as much as I want to hold you,
help you through

the pain and the shame and the disdain –
we cannot speak of it.

FIRESTORM

The wind blows plumes
over the peak,
drifting
like the fog of early morning,
yet now the sky turns red.
Where are you?
In the smoke I keep
looking for your escape.

Work

Angel Island, 1910 to 1940

IN THE FOG

Late in the afternoon,
he looks up from his desk.
Sunlight dapples in the fog.
He thinks of the lamb roast
his wife makes on Fridays.
Saturdays at the yacht club
sailing the bay with his son.
Last Sunday with his father
in his new house by the sea,
Angel Island a golden peak
glimpsed in the fog.
For the first time in his life
he saw the old man beam,
I'm proud of you, son.

*

A cable from Washington.
He picks it up and scoffs
at her tears,
her husband begging him
to let her bury their boy.
But it's the law.
She cannot be a citizen.
She cannot be landed.
She cannot be trusted.
He sends on the decision.
Denied.
No unusual hardship found.
This last task done,

he takes the ferry home.
In the fog he cannot hear
a woman wailing.

DAYDREAMS

He gets off the ferry at nine each day,
walks past the sea of yellow faces,
their worries creased into their brows.

He dreams of the girl he met last week
her sweet kisses, her blond tresses,
the skin at the back of her thigh.

He picks up the papers on his desk,
scans for the name, the final decision,
the tales inside just words to him.

He looks at the photograph in the file,
a woman gazing stiffly past the lens,
as if dreaming of a distant paradise.

In her eyes he sees his mother
fleeing a homeland plagued by famine,
huddled on Ellis Island.

AT THE INTERVIEW

Before he came to Angel Island
he roamed *from sea to shining sea,*
hauling grain, mining coal.

Here the work is steady.
His back no longer screams
as he rolls out of bed each day.

He has a wife, too, a fine woman
who looks at him with longing
as their child stirs inside her.

But this morning he met a widow
with six young children in tow.
He wanted to hear her story,

give her a chance
to return to her family,
but the orders came from above:

The children can land. She's
likely to become a public charge.
He looked away as she cried.

BLOODLINES

He wanted to be an engineer,
finished at the top of his class,
but despite his ease with English,
he could not find a job.

This work isn't what he wanted.
He has to split his loyalties
between the country of his birth
and the motherland he never knew.

The white men distrust him.
The Chinese see him as a traitor.
Like men who sign up for war,
he begins to see himself as American.

This morning he had to tell a woman
the inspectors think she's a whore.
He stammered on his words
as she shifted her gaze to the floor.

In her eyes he saw his parents
fresh off the boat, bringing with them
the taint of blood that shaped his life
and brought him to this prison.

OFF THE RECORD

It's not her job to discern the lies,
only to write down what they say.

Her hand dashes across the page,
recording the facts of their lives -

grandmothers, grandfathers
brothers who left a year ago

the rice bin in the family home
the number of steps to the front door.

She pauses to wonder why
nine out of ten children are boys.

But in her industry she does not see
the verses they write on the walls,

their tears tossing in the surf,
the truths they cast into the fog.

HOUSEKEEPING

Words
on the walls,

brushed in ink,
carved on wood,

a language she
does not know.

She has just
begun to write

jumbles
on the page,

unsure
of what to say.

She looks
at these women

knitting
as they wait,

weaving,
unmaking,

their words silent
in their throats.

MEDICAL EXCLUSION

From the corner of his eye
he watches her take off her dress,
her eyes lowered, her face pale,
the cleft soft between her legs.

He reads her chart and shivers,
hookworm, possibly syphilis,
the lines she has already crossed,
the dirt under that lustrous skin.

ACTS OF FAITH

The women recite with her,
their voices rising and falling,
tongues tangled in words
they have yet to understand.
Thou shalt not misuse the name
of the Lord your God.
She watches the girl in the corner,
silent, her eyes
drifting toward the sea.
She wants to tell her
of the land of the free,
a kingdom of believers,
where sinners become saviors.
But she knows no words
can salve a child lost to fever,
no words can allay
an eternal prison.

SHORE LEAVE

On his day off
he goes to the city,
stops by a grocery,
picks up peanuts
already split open,
stuffed with notes,
the shells glued back.
On the island
he sneaks them
into the pork slop
and they pay him
for the deceit.
With the money
he goes to the city,
reclines on a lounge,
inhales the smoke
of refined poppies,
and tries to forget
the misery he sees.

VIGILANCE

No matter how many times
he tries to erase their words,
painting over the black strokes,
filling the crevices with putty,
they keep writing their verses
in a language he'll never know,
defacing the blank slate
he works so hard to create.

Riot

San Francisco, July & August 1877

CITY HALL

I see him in the sandlots,
his voice fiery,
his eyes raised to the sky.

His lips curl into a sneer.
He flings off his coat
and unbuttons his collar.

And whatever happens,
the Chinese must go!
And the crowd cheers.

I see a young man raise his fist.
Once he built the railroads,
now he waits in pantry lines.

I see a man with a pickaxe.
The children at home
have no food to eat.

I see a woman in a corner.
Her husband's doused
in the drink of despair.

They think of those people
who take away their jobs,
who speak a language

they cannot understand,
who live in tenements
and send their money home,

who eat dogs and rats
and spend their nights alone
in a haze of sweet smoke,

and they think of his words,
And no matter what happens,
the Chinese must go!

I see him again in the sandlots,
a boy of eleven without a father,
trying to make a living at sea,

each year drifting farther
from the home he had to leave,
knowing he will never return.

ANTICIPATION

In his fatigues he looks
almost like a soldier.
Men outside
gather in the sandlots,
standing
in solidarity
with their compatriots
back east
who were *given*
a rifle diet,
their bodies sliced
by bayonets.
Called up for duty,
not yet deployed,
he waits in the armory,
standing
at attention
as the officers bellow.
I watch him
twitch his fingers
and wonder who
he will defend the city
against:
the strikers
or the Chinese?

NOB HILL

Behind the walls of his mansion
he holds his boy close.

Nine years ago he placed
the child on a silver platter,

displayed to a hundred guests
and his convalescing wife.

Outside, men smash windows,
spill rice onto the streets,

their fists now raised
toward the steamship docks.

I hear him tell the boy
he should count his blessings:

unlike those *dregs of Asia,*
he was born to a worthy people,

and unlike those hoodlums,
he must always strive.

He points beyond the sea.
One day all this will be yours.

He does not say that it was he
who brought in the Chinese

to build the railroad
that built this home atop the hill.

And he does not yet know
the boy would not become a man,

felled by a fever
in another, ancient land.

TO CHINATOWN

In speech after speech,
their voices raised to fever pitch,
they rail against the callous
cruelty of the men in suits
taking their land, taking their work.

A band marches up Market Street.
Speak, they sing. *Tell us*
how to drive out the Chinamen.
Shots ring from a balcony,
a man clutches his bloody knee.

Cracks of wood on flesh.
Someone's beating a Chinaman.
The crowd turns around,
their blood already churning,
but it's only two whites in a fight.

I don't notice him at first.
He watches from the edge
as a man on the podium warns
the police are on alert,
the militia under arms.

Maybe his wife just left him
in a string of shattered plates.
Maybe he's looking for
something beyond himself,
a crowd he can become.

Mass meeting! He hears the call.
The men around him roar.
He cannot make out what they say,
but the noises jolt his bones
and he moves toward the rumble.

WHAT HE SAID

I watch him dash into his shop,
slam the door, lock the bolt,

as the mob marauds down the street,
hurling rocks, shooting birds.

They were not after him,
but he's never felt this shaken,

no longer safe
in this city he calls home.

I hear him say aloud, as if to me,
The Chinese, the Chinese must go.

I may be Chinese, but
I've heard this said of others,

in whispers of confidence as if
I agree in my blood.

IMMOLATION

They found him in an alley
foaming at his mouth.
The sweet smell of poppies
lingered in his breath.

They cut the head off a duck,
put its neck down his throat,
pumped its blood into his body,
an old Chinese remedy.

The neck slipped out,
spraying his face with blood
already congealing
as he breathed his last.

The mob had sieged his shop,
broken down the doors,
chased him out with sticks,
and set it all ablaze.

What were his thoughts
when he took the opium,
knowing it would bring him
to his end?

Did thoughts of failure rise
from the shadows of his heart
and remind him of the home
he had fled?

Did thoughts of a return
fill him with dread and shame
and push him
over the edge?

HER STORY

I cannot seem to find her story.
She had been lured by the promise
of a rich man in America,
but when she landed on these shores
she was made to strip
and sold to the highest bidder.
Four years she must work without wages
to pay the price of her passage.
She gets ten days off a year,
a month's more work for ten days of sickness,
not enough to cover the days
her blood flows.
She cannot leave
until she pays off her debt.
What happened to her
when the mob came marauding?
Did men beat her,
have their way with her,
a fallen woman
who cannot fall lower?
If I don't tell her story
we cannot see her,
and without a reason for her being,
how will we let her survive?

HEADLINE

I see him in his office,
pacing by his desk,

trying to write the news.
He cannot fathom

these two days and nights
of mayhem and rage.

The workingmen only
want a fair wage

for an honest day's work.
They are good men like him,

trying to make a living
and go home to those

they cherish and love.
The Chinese question

must be settled,
but only in peaceful ways,

at the ballot box
and giving their jobs back

to the worthy.
But those hooligans

inflamed with liquor
and their own evil passions -

He stops and writes,
The Hoodlum Riot.

LITTLE SHADOWS

She cannot confront him
for without his good name,
she has nothing.

She thinks of those women
whose filthy blood
now mingles with her own.

She mutters
as she looks in the mirror,
The Chinese must go.

DELIVERANCE

He gathers the stories
he hears from his voters,
tales of lost jobs, hungry children,
wayward fathers, broken homes,
a city unsafe to live in.
He vows to go to Washington
and get their voices heard,
for the Chinese, the Chinese must go.

Pilgrimage

To get to Angel Island, I board
a ferry, cross the cold bay waters

once a fence to keep out
the jailbirds of Alcatraz. I watch

seagulls take off, their white wings
beating toward the city. At the prison,

I hear the sea lap the crumbling shore.
I read the words on the walls, almost

faded into the wood, penned
in a language I no longer understand.

Yet I feel their rhythms in my body,
whispering their tales to me, straddling

the shifting coast in this faraway land,
where I take up my pen and imagine

the borders we inhabit, the borders
we inherit, and in writing this story

I find my way home.

Notes

THE ANGEL ISLAND POEMS

In 1970, California State Parks ranger Alexander Weiss entered an abandoned building on Angel Island. The state wanted to demolish these ruins and turn the cove into a recreational playground. But when Weiss turned on his flashlight, he saw writings on the walls, some brushed in ink, others carved into the wood. He did not understand the language, but he knew the island's history and surmised that Chinese detainees had written these words.

Weiss reported his find to his supervisors, but they dismissed the writings as mere graffiti. He disobeyed his bosses and brought his discovery to George Araki, a professor he knew at the San Francisco State College. Araki's mother had spent time on the island as a Japanese picture bride. He brought the photographer Mak Takahashi to document the writings. Most of them, they found, were poems.

Most of the poems were written in colloquial Cantonese and used classical Chinese forms. Each line has the same number of words, usually five or seven, and each poem four or eight lines. A few are longer. The poets did not always follow the strict meters and rhyme schemes of the traditional forms.

Most of the poems were untitled and unsigned.

In the early 1930s, on separate occasions, Jann Mon Fong and Tet Yee copied poems while in detention and carried them to San Francisco when they landed. Each man recorded more than ninety poems, about seventy of which overlap. These, together with the Takahashi photographs, make up the majority of the 135 poems we now have on record.

All these poems were found in the men's barracks. The women's quarters were destroyed in the 1940 fire that shuttered the immigration station.

A HISTORY OF CHINESE IMMIGRATION IN AMERICA

1875 Page Act: First federal immigration law. This act prohibited the continued entry of contract laborers and Chinese women suspected of prostitution. Before a woman left for America, she had to submit a statement of personal morality to the U.S. consulate in Hong Kong. She also had to appear for an interview, during which she was asked about her sexual past. When she arrived in America, she was asked the same questions and her appearance matched to the photographs sent ahead from Hong Kong.

1877 San Francisco Riot: A labor rally in the sandlots next to City Hall devolved into two days of mob violence in Chinatown. The following month, Denis Kearney founded the Workingmen's Trade and Labor Union of San Francisco on an anti-Chinese and anti-capitalist platform, advocating the use of violence to meet political goals.

1882 Immigration Act: Denied admission to immigrants deemed liable to become a public charge, regardless of race or gender. Those with physical or mental illnesses that rendered them unfit to work, as well as unmarried pregnant women, fell into this category. Chinese women not supported by husbands or fathers were excluded on the grounds that they were unlikely to find work and might resort to prostitution.

1882 Chinese Exclusion Act: Aimed at banning the entry of Chinese laborers, this law made exceptions for merchants, diplomats, teachers, students, tourists, returning U.S. citizens, and their immediate families. Chinese who claimed to be merchants had to show financial records and business contracts.

Those who claimed to be family were questioned on their knowledge of the relationship. This legislation also denied all Chinese the right to naturalization.

1892 GEARY ACT: Extended the Chinese Exclusion Act. It also required all Chinese in the U.S. to carry a certificate of residence at all times.

1906 SAN FRANCISCO EARTHQUAKE: Destroyed City Hall and all birth, marriage, and citizenship records. Many Chinese made false claims to U.S. citizenship and America could not disprove them. A federal immigration judge said that if all these claims were true, then each Chinese woman in America before 1906 would have had 500 children. Chinese merchants and U.S. citizens also claimed unrelated men as their sons. Brokers in San Francisco drew up coaching papers that detailed fictitious family histories, which these "paper sons" memorized and told the immigration officers.

1910 ANGEL ISLAND IMMIGRATION STATION: Modeled after Ellis Island, its location in the San Francisco Bay was thought to prevent escape, families sneaking coaching information to detainees, and the spread of infectious diseases. Some of the Chinese, who had the longest detentions, wrote poems on the barrack walls.

1917 IMMIGRATION ACT: Instituted a literacy test for adult immigrants and extended the exclusion laws to the Asiatic Barred Zone, which included Japan, India, and most of Southeast Asia.

1921 EMERGENCY QUOTA ACT: Aimed at restricting the influx of immigrants from southern and eastern Europe, this act instituted quotas by national origin.

1924 Immigration Act: Aimed at the total exclusion of immigrants from Asia, this act denied admission to all "aliens ineligible for citizenship." In particular, it excluded the foreign-born wives of Chinese merchants and U.S. citizens. In 1925, the U.S. Supreme Court ruled to allow merchant wives. In 1930, the high court ruled that the wives of U.S. citizens could be admitted only if the marriage occurred before the law passed.

1940 Angel Island Immigration Station: A fire destroyed the administrative building and the women's barracks. The immigration station closed and the detainees were moved to a San Francisco county jail.

1943 Magnuson Act: Repealed the Chinese Exclusion Act and instituted an annual quota of 105 Chinese immigrants.

1965 Immigration and Nationality Act: Abolished the system of quotas by national origin and instituted a preference system based on professional skills and family relationships.

BIBLIOGRAPHICAL NOTES

This book is a work of fiction, but the stories are rooted in historical fact. Some of the characters are based on real people, but their interior lives are my invention.

I relied on Erika Lee and Judy Yung's *Angel Island: Immigrant Gateway to America* (Oxford University Press, New York, 2010) for the historical overview, the technicalities and implications of the immigration laws, the material conditions on the island, and many of the individual stories.

I also referred to Him Mark Lai, Genny Lim, and Judy Yung's *Island: Poetry and History of Chinese Immigrants on Angel Island, 1910 - 1940* (HOC DOI Project, San Francisco, 1980; University of Washington Press, Seattle, 1991) for oral histories and translations of the poems found in the men's barracks. To date, this is the most comprehensive anthology of the surviving Angel Island poems.

I used the *San Francisco Chronicle* archives to reconstruct the stories of the San Francisco Riot of 1877.

In the Afterword to *Ludlow* (Red Hen Press, Los Angeles, 2007), a verse-novel of the 1914 Ludlow Massacre in the southern Colorado coalfields, poet David Mason discusses the roles of fiction and verse in historical storytelling. He quotes Jorge Luis Borges, "I believe that the poet shall once again be a maker. I mean, he will tell a story and he will also sing it."

ACKNOWLEDGMENTS

I would like to thank the editors of the following publications, where some of these poems first appeared:

PANK: "In a Wooden Building," "The Waves," "The Walls Speak," "On the Boat," "Virtue Exam."

Pilgrimage: "Daydreams."

Poecology: "Off the Record."

Winter Tangerine Review: "Paper Son."

The poems in *Voices* were made into an artist book titled *The Walls Speak: Angel Island, California* in collaboration with Gail Watson of Birdwood Press. It was exhibited as part of *See & Say: A Symbiosis of Visual and Literary Art*, by invitation of the Art Students League of Denver and the Lighthouse Writers Workshop, at the Abecedarian Gallery in Denver, Colorado in May 2015.

I would also like to thank Chris Ransick, for your mentoring and reading of this manuscript; Andrea Doray, for your astute final edit of this manuscript; Lidia Yuknavitch, for showing me the permission I needed to give myself to write; Rae Gouirand, for seeing a book on Angel Island in my morass of words; Quinn Fairchild, for the early suggestion that shaped this book; Caleb Seeling and the team at Conundrum Press, for shepherding this book into the world.

And to the friends and family who shared scotch with me under the stars, who hiked and skied with me when the going got rough, who believed in me before I believed in myself: this would have been much harder without you.